HOLY
GROUNDS

JOHN BRIGHTMAN BROCK

HOLY GROUNDS

When God Shows Up, Everything Changes!

Trilogy Christian Publishers A Wholly Owned Subsidiary of Trinity Broadcasting
Network 2442 Michelle Drive Tustin, CA 92780
Copyright © 2020 by John Brightman Brock

Rights Department, 2442 Michelle Drive, Tustin, CA 92780.
Trilogy Christian Publishing/ TBN and colophon are trademarks of Trinity Broad-
casting Network.
For information about special discounts for bulk purchases, please contact Trilogy
Christian Publishing.
Trilogy Disclaimer: The views and content expressed in this book are those of the
author and may not necessarily reflect the views and doctrine of Trilogy Christian
Publishing or the Trinity Broadcasting Network.
Manufactured in the United States of America
10 9 8 7 6 5 4 3 2 1
Library of Congress Cataloging-in-Publication Data is available.
B-ISBN#: 978-1-64773-354-4
E-ISBN#: 978-1-64773-355-1

DEDICATION

This book is dedicated to my heavenly Father, who through His Son, my Lord Jesus, and His Holy Spirit has been guiding, guarding all the way.

PREFACE

THESE TIMES OF FAITH

John Brightman Brock is a veteran journalist of forty-three years, working as a state capital bureau reporter, political columnist, staff writer, city editor, and managing editor in various publications in Florida, Alabama, and Texas.

His last stint, of twelve years, was spent as managing editor of a blue ribbon award-winning weekly newspaper in South Florida. And when the industry started its transformation into digital publishing, so did Brock, as his newspaper morphed into a visually-driven weekly magazine appealing to all demographics, whether in print, online, or on social media.

Retiring recently from management and from freelance writing in other magazines at age sixty-four, it was a time to "be still and know that I am God," as Brock quotes from Scripture. It was a time to rest.

In his first book, *Holy Grounds*, Brock throws aside any lofty perspectives of a changing world of journalism, opting rather to examine his greater journey with God.

What does it all mean to be a Christian? Was I really chosen for some greater good?

What does God want with me, and why does He continually appear in our lives in stark, and many times humbling, situations?

How can I please this God, with His undoubtedly yet wonderfully controlling nature?

The author traces the answers to these questions, providing anecdotal memories peppered with a somewhat jaded humor but cultivated like a farmer, weaving into miraculous outcomes where God became his everlasting Friend.

Read, enjoy, and identify, where applicable, with this happy child who grew to be a conservative teen, only to look evil in the face as a worldly adult caught in the daily dramas of the Christian life.

His hope is that you see there's more to the abundant life than salvation. That's just a glorious beginning.

The day-to-day living in this world, where we operate as "strangers and pilgrims," is the challenge God sets before us.

But God, "who is rich in mercy," as Scripture describes Him, is there with you all along your journey.

And sometimes—in those at first fearful but ultimately sweet periods of all-out faith—God shows up right in front of you.

It's these miraculous times that Brock recalls as his "Holy Grounds."

GOD'S INVITATION TO "HOLY GROUNDS"

When Mel Gibson's monumental film *The Passion of The Christ* first came out, it reignited my spiritual life and jumpstarted my professional career in Palm Beach County, Florida. At nearly the same time, a published book added more of the same divine guidance, in Pastor Rick Warren's *The Purpose Driven Life: What on Earth Am I Here For?* Now spiritually "armed to the teeth," as the saying goes, when I took over at a newspaper, the *Jupiter Courier* (and later magazine, the *Jupiter Courier Newsweekly*), in Jupiter, FL, publishers and friends became a godsend of direction to influence a community for God and His excellence.

My purpose was wonderfully manifested, contact by contact. And after our first year, our publication won the Florida Press Association's first place award for general excellence by weekly newspapers in our circulation category. God had shown the way.

That began the same year as my new marriage, 2006, when God had us reading the *Purpose* book nightly for years afterward. We began making waves spiritually with our families and friends. Although, many times we read with trepidation God's words through the author, in chapters that came to life before us. We wondered what would be required of us next. Scary? Well, yes. But awesome is our God.

It was kind of like Moses of biblical history meeting God in a burning bush, and his life suddenly getting a rocket-like purpose from that "Holy Ground."

I can only explain this new emphasis on direction as God's

"Holy Grounds" of confirmation wherever we went. My wife and I took a stand for the literal interpretation of the Bible everywhere—and nearly everywhere, especially in our private lives, the pushback from evil was evidenced by those whom we soon labelled "border bullies," but who ultimately gave way to God's direction. Many battles, but all victories. God was batting a thousand percent.

It took me back to the "Holy Ground" I first experienced when I was seven years old. Once I accepted God's way of revealing Himself to me, these extraordinary situations have been commonplace.

"God extends His love to us…"

One afternoon, I walked into my parents' room in Aiken, SC, and crawling up on the bed with Mama, *I asked her to explain God to me. John 3:16 (KJV) was the answer: "For God so loved the world, that He gave His only begotten Son, that whosoever believeth in Him should not perish, but have everlasting life."*

She told me of God's love, and I began to have the first saving knowledge of my sinfulness, even at that age, and knew that I needed to personally accept His Son Jesus as my Savior from my own sins—because separation from God had been the result.

A few nights later at Levels Baptist Church in Aiken, I was there in a pew alone, while my parents were seated not too far away. It was one of those Southern Baptist revivals, not unlike those you've seen pictured in so many films. Strong Bible Scripture rang through from the pulpit to my little head and heart. Hallelujah! This time, my first "Holy Ground" experience with our Lord, is indeed the dearest in my memory.

I've heard of parents being fearful of explaining to children the concept of good and evil, sin and righteousness, hell, and heaven's salvation. But I'm here to tell you: whether or not God's story is told outright, God will reach them with that message of salvation and reunion with the Creator. Meanwhile, Satan also uses every tool he can to capture their souls. The battle is on.

Such was the intensity in my pew as I listened to the altar call to "come forward and profess your faith in the Lord Jesus Christ as your personal Savior and Lord," as the preacher said from that pulpit. I looked up and saw it straight ahead, but it felt like miles to walk down to the front.

As the altar call began, I knew that it was for me—what Mama had said would be "God's call on my life."

I got up from my seat and turned determinedly to the left for entry into the long aisle down to the front. But then, as vividly as anything has ever been in my memory, an actual presence said to me: "Sit down," coaxing me to forget the words of invitation. It was like a weight on me—and so, frightened, I sat down.

Perplexed, I now wasn't aware of where my parents were, or where the minister was, or even the pulpit at this point. *What's going on?* I thought. And I felt small at the awareness of two separate messengers battling—for me, it seemed.

But then a small voice, which I have wonderfully come to know now for almost sixty years, calmed my fears, nearly taking me by the hand as I was lifted up out of my seat—this time unafraid. I knew in whom I was now believing, and that this was my "invitation," from Jesus and from the pastor, to tell the world that I had believed, and who now owned my soul.

Time sped up as I walked down front and did the seemingly miraculous. Later, facing the congregation, and standing with my smiling six-foot-six Daddy behind me with both hands on my skinny shoulders, I pushed that little confrontation with evil out of my mind. Strangely, one of my second-grade classmates came up to me and asked, "Do you feel any different?"

I said, "No." But God and I knew that the battle had been won back in the pew.

This milestone of milestones, this rebirth into life everlasting, started building from that point onward in the journal being written of my own purpose driven life.

"Into my heart…"

Anecdotally, weeks later, one of my three older sisters and I were riding bicycles one afternoon, and up ahead on that long street, a neighbor's dog began to bark. He sounded big. He was big—and on a chain, I hoped, as my sister pedaled far ahead and faster, past that dog and his bared teeth.

I didn't stop this time as I felt like a veteran, of sorts, of conflict in my little world. I remembered my rebirth words—those from a popular children's song—and started singing to myself, first softly, as I pedaled, then louder and louder as I approached the dog and rode past him.

I've enjoyed repeating those words often through the years, when fears of evil and calamity have appeared. Subsequently, God's victories have peppered my life with more of His "Holy Ground" victories. I keep wanting to just take my shoes off and revel in Him.

Dear words from that song, "Into My Heart," by Harry D. Clarke: "Into my heart, into my heart/Come into my heart, Lord Jesus/Come in today, come in to stay/Come into my heart, Lord Jesus."

Always works.

GOD SHOWS UP!

Some of the most comforting yet commanding promises God gave us in His Word are found in Scripture references such as, "it is God who worketh in you," "the battle is the Lord's," or "be still and know that I am God."

Then there are those like, "I can do all things in Christ Jesus," "say things that are not as if they are," "without faith it is impossible to please God," or "He shall give his angels charge over you."

So, what's a Christian to do? Wait, or do?

Jesus provides the answer.

He was always "about My Father's business," as He told His mother once. Because of Jesus' obedience to the Father to the point of death, ours is merely to commune with God, walking and talking with Him as we were first created, as in a place once called Eden.

Because of Christ's salvation of our souls from the curse of sin, God wants simply for you to "know Him and the power of His resurrection." And God *will* draw near to you as you draw near to Him.

Places of communion with our Holy God, or as I like to call them, "Holy Grounds," confirm His love to us in that He wants to know us integrally.

And our part? Be ready to respond with gratitude for this relationship and appreciation for what He has done. The next step requires resting in our role of obedience, service, submission, humility, and… reliance on His infinite strength.

Meanwhile, on our *Late Great Planet Earth*, as author Hal

Lindsay once titled a book about our testing grounds, we can look forward to the future—with praise to our God.

I even like to brag—or boast—about my Father around Christians and non-Christians alike. Scripture states that "He inhabits the praises of his people." It also states that "His Word does not return unto Him void." With this eternal backup, I might add, "the sword of the Spirit" is a handy-dandy weapon to spiritually face our foe.

As a mustard seed…

In the many, many dire situations of need in my life through which God surely has been watching, a quick "Help me, Jesus!" somehow activated His power as "an ever-present help in time of need." Amen.

Back in the day, I was known as "the bone" in my late teens—at six-foot two-inches and with a weight far below the norm, "the most gangly-looking boy I've ever seen," my high school basketball coach once said, addressing me like a drill sergeant, looking me up and down in front of my teammates.

When I sometimes took center court for the game's first jump ball, fans, family, friends—and, I must confess, me too—were mindful that my maroon bottoms might not stay on my person if I jumped too high. I was not beyond holding my left hand on the waistband, as I recall. And I asked Jesus for His help in those games.

So, the Lord later—somehow—made me actually well-known for a fade-away jump shot that I developed with the Cougars. Funny how the Lord's strength "perfected in your weakness," as Scripture says, had a new meaning for this tall, skinny kid.

A few years earlier God had shown up, this time imparting faith in exchange for my weakness. It was a memorable "Holy Ground" of His power.

I was a young boy, just a week out of getting my braces off, and Daddy wanted me to try out for Little League in Waynesboro, VA, where we lived for eight years. The team coaches were there to pick who would go to which teams in an effort to form a good season for fans to watch, kids to grow, and advertisers to be promoted. All for our development.

But that particular tryout day was hot, steamy… and pop-up flies were not about to show my forte for catching and fielding that little white ball.

Thinking back to that day, I recall that a good distance away, a coach "popped up" a ball into the sky for me to catch. I was next in a long line of kids trying out, with scores of parents watching. But the sun and the ball became one in that expanse of blue sky, and all I remember was putting my glove up toward both.

It's hazy to remember, but I do know that I later woke up in a hospital emergency room with a broken nose and broken teeth. But when Daddy took me home, Mama "let me have it," as my sisters would say, for ruining the expensive and perfect smile that would never be the same.

His mercy has influence…

"But God, who is rich in mercy," to quote a Scripture passage, evidently had influence on the Moose Club Athletics coaches, who took me on as a pity case to fill out their roster. After all, it must have been a choice between this skinny boy not making a team, and somehow making up for his bloody injuries.

That year was God's own *Field of Dreams* (to reference a much later movie by Phil Alden Robinson, adapting W.P. Kinsella's *Shoeless Joe* novel) for me in my green and gray Athletics uniform. Coaches at first put me in right field, hoping that no balls would be hit in that area. Home plate always loomed large to me.

Scared? Yes, so scared at each at-bat that I was known for closing my eyes and saying, "Help me, Jesus," under my breath and mouthing my words. Daddy always watched from the fenced grandstand, behind home plate.

As preposterous as it sounds, home plate in that little park became the Lord's "Holy Ground" for me, as that season of fear turned into a season of faith.

Each time, asking Jesus with my same words of request—and closing my eyes and swinging—somehow, I connected to the ball. Amazing, as I recall. And to Daddy in the stands.

At season's end and at our Moose Club awards presentations, I was noted to have been the player "without an ounce of fat," the description read. More notably to me, and to Daddy, was that I was the one player who now led the entire Little League in hits. Glory to God.

The Lord loves to show off, I must add, in that my last at-bat came with my same "Help me, Jesus." As a definite show of God's strength, my "blind" bat connected for a homerun over the center field fence. Hooray! The dugout erupted on the infield and my teammates gathered at home plate—God's new "Holy Ground," at least in my life, where He had showed up in my time of need.

The kids were wild with excitement to pat my skinny self and blue helmet with congratulations.

"Don't hit his face," a doctor in the stands yelled, sitting not far from Daddy. I heard him yell that, as I rounded second. Actually, my broken nose had healed a little, and my two new caps on my front teeth gave me that seasoned, hayseed look—for a kid. I smiled.

I still wear that smile proudly.

Proud of God, and a "Holy Ground" at home plate.

HIS SWEET, SWEET SPIRIT

Thanks to the overwhelming love of our Father God, the exponential grace of his Son, the Lord Jesus, and the river of comfort of the Holy Spirit, our lives in this "veil of tears," as the Apostle Paul called earth, can turn divinely sweet when our "Holy Grounds" materialize in front of us.

As with God's directive to Moses upon seeing the biblical burning bush—to take off his shoes on Holy Ground—our own "grounds" can become similar milestones of communion with God.

These places provide respites from battles, times of solace away from Satan, or newfound empowerment from our Lord. Recognizing these supernatural "Holy Grounds" is, like other spiritual discernment gifts, like turning on a light bulb, ushering in a "Sweet, Sweet Spirit" in this place, to quote a Bill and Gloria Gaither song.

We may find ourselves standing in these places in times of tragedy, pain, or loss, including death. "To be absent from the body is to be present with the Lord," Scripture tells us, pointing to the ultimate "Holy Ground" of heaven.

In my life, witnessing the passing of saints has provided a sweet portal to their journeys' commencement. I was allowed to be a part of these "homecomings" for my grandmother, Rebecca Garrett McWhorter, in 1973, and more than forty years later, my mother, Florence McWhorter Brock.

Had I been quicker to discern these events as "Holy Grounds," my shoes would have been off and I would have been kneeling—whether at eighteen or fifty-nine.

"Cloud of witnesses" and me…

I don't recall the Lord preparing me for these two passings, but in each case, their deaths were preceded by a completeness of their purpose.

My grandmother was hospitalized in the last stages of pneumonia, simultaneous to the family-searing divorce of my parents waning in a courtroom not far away. It was essential that she outlive the proceedings, in order to allow many of my mother's birth family assets to continue without loss to a marriage gone awry.

On the final day of that courtroom drama, Mama and I returned to Grandmother's hospital room bedside after the final ruling in Mama's, and Grandmother's, favor.

"It's okay now, Mother," Mama said to her mom, who was lying face-up with her eyes closed and with raspy, painful breathing and great effort. "You've won, Mother. I'm okay now. You can go home to be with the Lord."

I listened, speechless, as Grandmother, who had been a beacon of my Southern Baptist training for years, did not open her eyes or show any sign of acknowledgement. I felt helpless. She just kept up that labored breathing as we both kissed her goodbye, not knowing that it would be the last time the three of us would be together on that bedside "Holy Ground." But God did.

We drove home, a few miles away.

Within minutes of our entering the house, the kitchen phone rang and a hospital nurse told Mama, "Your Mother has gone." We turned on our heels and were back at her bedside within fifteen minutes.

Mama held Grandmother's hand, and I placed my hand on

Grandmother's forehead. Strangely, at least to my knowledge, it was cooler, but with a slight warmth still there. But this time, Grandmother didn't breathe at all, and her entire upper body was lunged upward in bed in what appeared to be a final exhale. Awesome, the power of God!

"He will lift you up…"

Fast forward through the decades, as my wife and I became caregivers for the caregiver: Mama, who was to live with us, or in memory care facilities, for five years. She passed on to heaven at age ninety-one.

Alzheimer's is a debilitating disease which, among other things, slowly robs sufferers of their recent memories and leaves them reveling in fonder memories of childhood, and ultimately the mind's control over even present-day life loses its grip as well.

Thank the Lord for patient primary care physicians, specialists, adult day care registered nurses, and especially the kind hearts of hospice, who called early one morning saying that Mama had passed. We arrived in her hospice room twenty minutes afterward and talked to Mama, even though we believed her spirit was already in transit. We spoke out loud just the same, and called relatives about her passing using the telephone by her bed.

I had talked to Mama by her bedside earlier that day, as she lay in a state of near death. I had become used to visiting her and carrying on a one-sided conversation with Mama, who by then had lost control of her ability to swallow water, eat food, or speak. She seemed so much smaller, curled up in a near fetal position on her left side. But I couldn't escape the feeling of God with me and Mama again… this time, for her passing.

I write this with all candor when I mention that a sweet Spirit had filled the room that afternoon.

Strangely wonderful was the scene as she lay there in her bed, eyes closed, forcing out her moans of confirmation as I spoke loudly the individual names of all of her family, extended family members, church friends, and others who loved her. It was quite a long list... but she somehow was allowed by God to "remember" each name, and to let me know it.

Such was the grace of God.

The scene a few days before in our residence had been dramatic, as the Lord helped us deal with Mama's final departure scenario. Friday morning, I received a call from her RN adult day care that she was having an episode with her Alzheimer's. Heading there, I called her doctor, who told me to take her immediately to hospice. But from Friday to Saturday evening there was "no room" in several counties' hospice facilities. Mama's state of anxiety and agitation back in our home was constant and around the clock, and a reason to ask God to intervene. And He did.

A room was found Sunday in Stuart, FL, not far from a newspaper where I worked.

But earlier, as we sat on the bed in our home with Mama, who couldn't speak—she could only wave her arms—it was a time to remember.

Looking back, in those final precious hours before the ambulance arrived to take her to hospice, Mama, my wife Mady Lee and I were allowed to share a special "Holy Ground" of God's miraculous provision. I explained what was about to happen, and that she was going to hospice, followed by us in our vehicle... and that she was soon going home to the Lord. The words were similar to those she had spoken to her mother years earlier.

Miraculously, she quickly turned to my wife, calling her "sweet girl," and to me she said, "I love you." Then she returned to the agitated state, and later the paramedics arrived. Then she was on her way to hospice, and in four days after that initial one, she was in heaven.

"But God, who is rich in mercy," as Scripture says, had given me two "Holy Grounds" to remember and cherish, from two women who had painstakingly trained me in understanding the rights and wrongs of life. Although in different rooms, in cities 150 miles apart, the atmospheres were similar—and the outcomes wonderfully the same.

"If you know the Lord, you need nobody else to see you through the darkest night." This is a line from the song "If You Know the Lord" by Bickley Reichner, and recorded in my youth by George Beverly Shea.

A DEMON IN MY VIEW

I have often thought that we Christians don't pay enough attention to our actual presence in this world.

For surely, the enemy does.

To prepare for our daily incursions into the world, our confidence remains in the Word of God.

Upon receiving the Lord Jesus Christ as our personal Savior and Lord, we receive the Holy Spirit inside our bodies—because He said so. In so doing, we then are and have "the righteousness of God in Christ"—because He said so. Our minds must be renewed each day with these basics.

In the spiritual realm, also, I believe the glory of God is not only in, but also around us. Surely, the very glory of God shows up when we do, and "pings" our presence in locations as we appear on the devil's radar.

Strange as it seems, his tracking device alerts his agents, invisible or visible. Got it? So, remind your brain tomorrow morning when your feet hit the floor.

"Twenty-four and so much more…"

In my early professional life I had lived in Central Florida and on the Texas-Mexican border, but when I arrived in Mobile, AL, at age twenty-four, I had not seen intense spiritual battle. It was, though, a coming of age not unlike Neil Young's popular song "Old Man," and its lyric "twenty-four and so much more."

The world was my oyster, as the saying goes, and Mobile had plenty of that shellfish, and scores of tough challenges for this writer to fill newspaper pages for the next fifteen years.

But that first week was strangely dark—a rite of passage, so to speak—and a revelation of sorts, when I got off work one midnight and went food shopping, looking sentimentally for some Pepsodent tooth powder, a brand my grandfather had used.

I'm sure I appeared a little vulnerable and naive in my journalist attire, but unknowingly I was observed to be more than just a shopper, but a child of the living God with the marks of salvation. But the ensuing abruptness and subtle confusion assaulting me from the evil one could have knocked me over with a feather.

In the natural scope of things, a cute store clerk about my age was stocking shelves near me, and I asked her where the tooth powders were. Her response—straight from a demonic source—lasted about fifteen minutes; a blur of spiritual intrusion and attack that carried my mind time-traveling in my defense. It was one of those "you'd have to be there to believe it" moments. My first such dilemma.

This young woman, whose name I won't use, actually gave me her personal testimony of Satan's power. She praised the someone—and the power—that had brought her to that very spot to encounter me.

Forgetting the tooth powder request, she boldly addressed me as if she knew me. She, this person, actually didn't, but her master did.

"Why do you do that?" she asked.

"Do what?" I responded.

"Put yourself in between God and Satan," she firmly accused me.

No response followed on my end… just my blank, young Christian persona—a deer-in-the-headlights look at the first spiritual cannon fire on a holy battlefield. It had become, however, a "Holy Ground" of God's presence.

I didn't know that it would be my first face-to-face look at a demon-possessed young woman who said she was from Texas. And she looked it.

Kind of like a young wayfarer not unfamiliar with Harleys and rocky roads, she looked like the type you'd expect to meet in New Orleans and share a bowl of oyster gumbo. At the same time, she could smile while changing your truck's oil and adjust the struts and alignment. Her hands were noticeably ruddy.

My whirling observations had to stop. I had to get quickly into this battle, and all I had were some Bible verses to attest to a conservative Christian home rearing. *But I'm saved,* I knew in my heart. And I had the Holy Spirit.

"You think that as a Christian, you're God!" she accused me, again speaking slowly so that I could feel the caustic gloom accompanying the words. *Wow,* I thought—her tones would have peeled the very paint from Granddaddy's bathroom wall. It was so chillingly abrupt.

"I believe in Jesus…"

How does she know my beliefs and can she be so bold to say this? I thought. *Well, I'm glad it shows—but man!*"No, I don't. I believe in Jesus," I countered.

"I know you do," she flashed back, looking busy with the product shelving items. "Not me. I gave my life to the other one… when he saved me as I was dying. I had been on my motorcycle and was pinned beneath a vehicle."

"He was there, the devil?" I asked.

"It was his presence, offering me life. And I took it," she said casually. "Still do." She smiled and moved away from that aisle, busying herself with other shelf stocking.

"You've got to get away from him, cross over to my side," I followed her, continuing. And she looked down, shaking her head. As the intensity seemed to pause, I got out of there. That was enough for me—my physical heart, my spiritual soul, and a Crusader mind seemed to urge me to find safety.

For the next few weeks, we became adversarial acquaintances, if you can say that. Sounds enticingly weird, I know. A strong pull is a better description. A mission.

I even once drove out to her mother's house where she lived, and witnessed the many cages of snakes in glass crates and the old sportscar she was working on. In that same bedroom community west of Mobile, a decade later, I would write stories about this very area where Satanic symbols were found on many of the young women, who said they didn't know how they got them. Allegations of witches' covens were rampant.

Looking back, it was after my first meeting with this grocery store clerk that I determined to point her to the Lord. In my apartment nearby, I'd play my guitar to the Lord and read my Bible in the afternoons before going to work for the night. She actually showed up several times, when I prayed earnestly, asking that God save her soul from the evil she worshipped.

"I know what you're doing!" she said angrily once, as she knocked on my K-7 apartment door. "You're praying for me, and you've got to stop. My looks can put a curse on you!"

Of course, I summoned up my spiritual toolbox of weaponry and said, as clearly as I could, looking into her eyes but addressing the demons inside: "I refuse your curses in the name of Jesus."

It was a phrase first spoken from my lips that I've found myself saying in many situations since. The power that I feel, and that I know happens, gives me an even stronger position of strength against the enemy.

I didn't see her for months after that, until some friends of mine met after work for late night drinks and eats at a local tavern. And there she was, of all the people to be our waitress, still looking as wayfaring as ever, as if the very wind blew her there. I had to ask her one question.

No crossing over...

"Did you ever become a Christian?" I asked her, standing up.

"Nope. He wouldn't let me cross over," was her last response to me. I sat back down and was sad, just sad.

Through the years, I have recalled that spiritual battle often, my "Holy Ground" of God's help when evil knew my name... and history.

Admittedly, it had been so invigorating to me—that very first meeting—that I had driven to my apartment, gotten out of my Toyota Corolla, and climbed to a hill overlooking the apartment complex. I had looked upward to my heavenly Father and the stars that He had made. On my back in the grass on that hill, I thanked the Lord for allowing to be alive for that "Holy Ground" of conflict and to engage in battle with the other side of spirituality—the tormented ones who "choose" another.

We really are here to give directions to home, and to the Savior who paid the price for our salvation from sin.

God had helped me to "hold fast to the faith" when it counted, though I didn't like the closeness of the enemy and his knowledge of me.

My Christian life had been... just fun, before that.

Kind of wished I could go back. Too late.

ANGELS AMONG US

William Shakespeare once wrote: "All the world's a stage, and all the men and women merely players." That's a broad-brush way to conclude that we really are not our own, and have a role to play on earth.

As Christians, magnify that perception of life by a hundred times on our "stage." Accept it or not, it's there—a script in a sense, pre-written for those whose names are in the Lamb's Book of Life, as we undoubtedly are.

"My heart would have fainted…" as one of God's Old Testament champions once said upon realizing his drama unfolding. The passage continues: "…had I not believed to have seen the Lord in the land of the living." So said David, when beset with the passions and challenges of servanthood.

I read this exact verse one night in my empty rental house at age twenty-nine. But at the time I had no debts, hardly any possessions, and no marriage or divorce under my belt. A mere babe in the spiritual woods, I had no reason to fear the havoc— and brush with death—that was to befall me later. Truly, as one client once told me in her house, "Careful, 'cause the devil's out there." She was right.

The flipside of it all is that God, "who is rich in mercy," His Son, and His Holy Spirit are the nuclear-tipped arrows in our quiver. Added to that, the possibility of "entertaining angels unawares" is a comforting resource for those who draw close to the Father.

Life's ensuing warfare can be outrageous, unreasonable, and unprompted. So, taking hold of this spiritual promise, and others like it, directly changes the natural landscape we all live in.

So, "boys and girls for Jesus," as a high school classmate once called believers, know your Bible—and charge into this Christian life for ultimate victory. It takes, well, merely a stage—with you on it. Your lines will be prompted by the Holy Spirit as needed! And you're soon to find yourself... on your own "Holy Ground."

He will give His angels charge over you...

As I grew older, I should have noticed that my own stage was being set for a call to battle. Soon, I was to feel a little like David, who was "beset on every side" by the enemy, as he told the Lord in Psalms.

The observance of Mardi Gras occurs in New Orleans, the Mississippi Gulf Coast, and Mobile, AL, for weeks before Lent, when confessions are quickly made for the open partying, and usually the offenders make some sacrifice—like not shaving facial hair—until Easter arrives.

For years, my newspaper reporter duties had me writing about the frivolity that accompanied the crowds lining the parade routes, when tipsy maskers aboard floats hurled boxes of Moon Pies and trinkets to outstretched arms below. Sometimes it was peaceful; other times the parade sheriff's deputies on horseback were tasked with more than crowd control. There were many shootings through the years when I covered that atmosphere. My only weapons were a police radio and a notepad; I also had a photographer.

In this season of winter festivities, late one night after my work shift ended at midnight, I had driven across the causeway over Mobile Bay but then ran out of gas. A trucker saw me in my knee-length wool coat, thumbing in the cold. He picked me up and said he had to deliver a load to the state docks area of the waterfront. It was a high-crime area, but it was the only chance I had to use a convenience store payphone to call for someone from my church group to bring me some gas.

After dropping me off at that little lit-up store, he watched me go to the payphone a few feet from the glass doors and trucked on his way. A half hour later, however, I lay faceup on the sidewalk by that same store doorway, the victim of a gang shooting that could have claimed my life. I remember him returning later, kneeling over me, crying, "I should have never let you off here. I'm so sorry."

On the phone, I had pleaded with someone to bring me some gas. I had paused, because one of several red-jacketed youths was suddenly pressing in on me from a foot away. "Can I help you?" I asked, rather agitated.

Placing a full clip of rounds in his pistol and pressing it onto my chest, he replied with expletives, "I'm fixing to show you what…" In retrospect, I realize from what police later said that it was a gang thing. I surmise that it was an initiation, and I—like others through the years—was the object that night.

"Help me…"

Something—or better yet, Someone—welled up inside me, and I turned my chest around from that weapon and placed my back up against it instead. Then I told myself, "I'm going to walk to the door, 'cause this isn't happening."

One step, two steps, and then the shot rang out. "Stop, b…" he yelled just before firing, as his gang members in two cars watched. But I wasn't there anymore. Call it being numb, or the determination to not be robbed at gunpoint; I had tried to exit the "scene." Sadly, his bullet "traced the bottom of my garment" as I like to say, and shattered a section of both bones below my left knee before exiting. I lay writhing in pain as my left leg gave out, feeling like rubber. I reached for my bones that were now unattached under the skin and in my grasp, in the literal pool of blood where I lay.

Yes—odd things do happen to Christians, and unsupposed evil. Still conscious, I crawled to the door and reached for that metal, horizontal bar. But the attendant came to the door, looked at me—then looked out at the several gang members outside—locked the door, and ran for cover. What would you do? Right—I yelled, "Call 911!"

Six months of hospital visits, wound treatment, an attempt at putting a rod in my leg, and decreasing lengths of leg casts transpired after that. During one of my hospital stays the police called, saying that some of the area's gangs were claiming responsibility for shooting an editor. Presented with the possibility of a mugshot lineup of the perpetrators, I declined... leaving them instead in the hands of my Lord, who has a way with vengeance.

Looking back at that night, the "scene" of the play unfolding took a heavenly turn in the next twenty minutes, as I lay there at the mercy of these bandits. I call it a "Holy Ground."

Realizing what I thought would be my fate, I let go of the door rail and lay on my back, looking up at the black sky instead of at the gang. Strangely, seeing the overwhelming, peaceful, eerie, silent evidence of God my Father there, I suddenly had hope. I yelled at the top of my lungs, "Father, help ME... Jesus, help ME... Holy Spirit, help ME!" I repeated those lines loudly, like it was the last scene of my life.

Not looking to the right or left, the solitude of it all was close. But the closeness of the Comforter was even more evident. Even peaceful.

In the stillness that followed, no gang member came upon me. The shooter ran to his carloads of buddies, and they watched... and left. There's no telling what they really saw.

Soon the paramedics arrived and tried to hold my arms from shaking, and they said they had no painkillers aboard, as was their policy in the area. Glad to be alive, but wracked with pain as we waited for the police to arrive, I was able to convince a lady paramedic to put a stick in my mouth for me to clamp down on to relieve the misery. I thought to myself, *There's no way I can stand this pain.* I was a different man after that. My colleagues at the newspaper's night shift all got some of those new "cell phones," and I started carrying a gun. I still have a problem with the challenge of making a tank of gas last, however.

And Mama got her wish, insisting, "You know you have to forgive that boy." And I did.

I've often since wondered: Are there really angels among us?

I believe that angels, to me "unawares," came to my side that night—and that they looked bigger, badder, and better-armed than my assailant and his gang.

One day in heaven, I'd like to see that "scene" from God's perspective.

SPIRITUAL SOUP DU JOUR

Many people of faith these days have become inquisitive enough to connect the dots of the Christian life.

It's a bold move that can reveal your personal, God-given power to talk like Jesus did, walk like He walked, and respond aggressively in actions as He did... all behind the enemy lines of a world pervaded by the prince and the power of the air. That's right—the old devil.

Sadly, happily, encouragingly, or sacrificially (whichever way you want to describe it), it all comes down to your faith to believe that He empowers you. And this, rather than running for your life when you realize that you've been personally targeted by intimidating, demonic forces. Your choice. Your testimony.

Need I say more?

Sometimes, if you're impassioned and even angry at this temporary ruler in your world, you can "be angry and sin not," to quote Scripture again, and again, and again. And win!

"Holy Ground" between the food aisles...

When I was in my mid-forties I was living in Panama City Beach, FL, a beach town that on spring break would bring hordes of rowdy college-age kids—and even high schoolers—to the beaches for weeks at a time.

Movies made to depict the often all-out raucousness of spring break, regardless of the country of origin, often pale in comparison to the unrestrictive partying that could go on at ground level, or on the twentieth floor high-rise condo decks, or inside the enormous beach bars at night, or at the raunchy pool competitions in the daylight—or even in a grocery store aisle across the beach highway, on one occasion.

Nothing was safe from the darkness on one particular spring night, for me especially, and it ended in a stand to spiritually fight on a different "Holy Ground."

I had the flu, and since I lived alone in a trailer three blocks off the beach with my three dogs, I had driven to a small chain grocery store and had seen one of my favorites—Campbell's mushroom soup. "Ah," I said to myself. "This should do the trick."

With can in hand in that lonely aisle, I was confronted—yes, confronted—by a roving band of late teen-aged boys, who had ambled across the highway to get some munchies to help them make it through the night. There were about eight of them, led by the smallest, most vocal mouthpiece from the "accuser of the brethren," again a quote from my Scripture memories.

"Wat'cha doing, ol' man?" he asked, stopping his pack of older teens who appeared nearly shoulder to shoulder and close enough to spit on, as an uncle of mine used to say.

The Holy Spirit has many descriptions, among them my favorite: "a River of power" that flows out of your innermost being. And for one Christian, standing on aisle four, it became a "Holy Ground" to take back from the devil. After all, it was better than spitting.

I stretched out my hand and put it on the leader's chest. He looked down at my hand, incredulous.

Acting quickly, but again not thinking in the natural, I attacked as Jesus would. "Praise the Lord Jesus Christ!" I demanded.

He looked at me like I had seven heads—and maybe I did. Or, just maybe, it was the seven attending angels around me and that can of soup. But then things turned in my favor.

The entire band of brothers, as it were, started marching—to my amazement. They forgot about me and passed me by, and loudly followed my command to the demons inside their bodies and around them. It didn't matter to me. I was winning!

But no joke, they marched up and down each aisle, and could be heard in the distance from my soup aisle, screaming, "Praise the Lord Jesus Christ! Praise the Lord Jesus Christ!"

All that was left in my aisle, though, was me... still holding onto my can of soup.

But I was—myself—praising the Lord Jesus Christ! Hallelujah.

So, I was happy to note this miracle as I looked down this grocery store aisle, wondering at just how many "Holy Ground" sites the Lord would claim in my life.

And I remembered, as I went out to my truck to drive back to my beach trailer, the Word of the Lord.

There really is power in the name of Jesus.

GIVE IT UP, FLESH!

The world, the flesh, and the devil. Ah, yes. These are "the enemies of our faith," according to Scripture.

Such was the Word of the Lord drummed into my every ear, every year, at church camps, Bible conferences, and Christian schools.

In the interest of transparency, to quote a phrase in our vernacular these days, it made many of us Christian teens more than just a little paranoid. Like when I was pulling out my guitar to entertain the girls at camp, I usually got a quick admonishment from a counselor upon witnessing my opportunity to shine with "Fire and Rain" by James Taylor. "Let's have a little more of the Lord, and a little less of Bubba," she'd say loudly, using my nickname, above my music.

Okay, so my talents were soon relegated to testimony times around the camp bonfire after that. I was good with that, too, as long as I kept ol' James' music under control.

But growing up through the years in God's grace—in God's bootcamp of the abundant life—the big three have become unmistakable, unrelenting, and unswayed antagonists for me, except for the power of the Holy Spirit.

God to the rescue, again.

So, for you God-described "mighty men of valor" out there— like Gideon—it's hard to keep confessing that our flesh gets in the way. And I don't mean just fleshly desires. I'm talking about that which wars against the Spirit. Our minds. Our reason. Our defenses. Our alibies. Yes… we're in a daily struggle.

Give it up, flesh. "Bring every thought captive" to the glory of

God.

Once, I had to trust the Spirit over my flesh—or die.

"Holy Ground" can be wet sometimes…

My "army of one" mentality was working hard on me years ago, when I still lived in a trailer off of Panama City Beach.

I'd get up early, just before the sun was coming up, and hit the beach running—yes, running—into the small surf and splashing hard with the first of a multitude of strokes, training my body hard, and swimming freestyle out into the vast Gulf of Mexico. What was I training for? Nothing, and everything. In my mid-forties, I still wanted to be a man for all seasons.

This mindset didn't even consider sharks, or trouble observed from would-be lifeguards or walkers on the beach. On that morning, there were none of either type.

My mind didn't even consider… drowning, for example.

It felt so good to defy the odds, breaking through the barriers of my muscle endurance, and to keep going as long as my arms could plow ahead and my legs could kick up a sea foam trail. I remember thinking, *Wow, this is great… but I've never done it this fast, this hard, and this far before.* As I plowed deeper into that water offshore, I could see the beach horizon over my left shoulder: the buildings, and the hazy gray dawn opening up the night skyline of beach cottages, restaurants, and amusements. Then, the beach scene trailed off as if non-existent, in my wake, with nothing else to glance at as I slammed my left arm over my head, splashing. Nothing but water.

And then the Lord spoke, not audibly like to Adam, Elijah, or Moses in biblical times, but in a Spirit message that pierced my no-limits mind: "What are you doing?"

I had been swimming hard for what seemed about thirty minutes. I had passed all the usual scenes I'd observed from shore. So, I stopped way out there—far out—past even where the big, rolling waves break in the distance. At first, I did some dog-paddling and looked around... but to my despair, I saw a far too distant shore, and even a miniscule beach, which frightened me to my core.

"Help me, Jesus," I screamed, not answering the question.

When you're that far out in the Gulf, you feel like a speck, and the waves are more than waves, they're a mass—monstrous, like mountains—something I had never, ever thought of before. Swimming back, at first very slowly, I tried to conserve my fleeting strength. In my rising fears, I was getting delirious about all that water. I remembered my interview years earlier with two survivors of a capsized boat, and their struggle to keep from drowning. One of them, wrapped in a U.S. Coast Guard towel, said about the Gulf, "It's the great hell."In my fears, I just stopped swimming.

I knew I was done...

For the first time in my life, my heart, my will, my mind—and yes, my flesh—gave up. The fear so gripped me that I knew I was done. "No way," I thought to myself. It wasn't just a feeling; I knew that I was going to drown. So, I started talking to God, as I knew that He knew exactly where I was, and that I was coming home to Him.

My arms stopped working and hung like lead weights on either side. I don't know what the medical term is, but they were totally incapacitated, so all I had was my torso, head, and legs. So, I just let myself go to the bottom, straight down... but I felt nothing, and so floated back up.

The Holy Spirit's message was, this time, not a question but a direction. To just turn on my back and look up at Him, where I was going—to take advantage of the "peace that passeth all understanding," according to Scripture.

"Forget about the waves. Forget about the shore," came His message. Amazed that I did not immediately drown, my deep breaths and the calmness of the Spirit unrealistically enabled me to just float… for what seemed like hours. Deep breaths continued to come in and exhale out. I was spread out like a starfish on that water.

The huge offshore waves, meanwhile, were carrying me toward shore. Occasionally I took a peek, but I tried not to even think anymore. But I would also occasionally jettison down toward the dark bottom of the deep water—nothing. Later, trying again, the same result. But then later, my left big toe found sea floor… and I pushed up. Trying again minutes later, ditto.

The distance was less and less to the bottom for that return push. I looked, and this time saw that I was actually closer to shore now—however, still south of the big waves that were my point of no return, I thought. My mind was slowly believing that God could make it happen.

The minutes passed, and the exercise continued until I was about fifty yards from shore, when I flattened out like an arrow and in freestyle forced those arms to move. I swam as hard as I could this time—coming ultimately to about ten yards from the surf, letting it carry me within ten feet of the dawning beach sand.

I just lay there, partially grounded, and dozing as the waves rolled over me as the sun came up. I fell asleep.

No one was on the beach; no problem. God and I were there. After a while, I got up and slowly walked up the street to my trailer. It was strangely surreal. I went into the bathroom, thinking that I might vomit in my exhaustion. As I looked into the mirror, I saw a sight I've never seen since.

Staring back at me was—it's hard to describe it other than as a frog man, with every fiber, every muscle in my neck, shoulders, waist, stomach, legs, calves, and feet seemingly exaggerated like a body builder's. Waking up hours later, I looked again, and my old self had returned. Had it all been a dream? No way. My swimsuit lay still wet in the shower, and I retained a deep lung cough for weeks from that "Holy Ground" experience in the Gulf.

The comforting Holy Spirit had kicked in when my mind— my flesh—had kicked out, failed me, left town, given up. In the giving up, His Spirit took over.

"The Spirit is willing, but the flesh is... weak," I remembered, from somewhere in my spiritual archives.

A shame we can't just give it up before God proves that His strength, His grace, is sufficient.

Can I get a good "Amen"?

A LITTLE FAITH

When you live in the woods on a riverbank, miles from no-where, you know that once you're there... you're there.

It's too far to drive back twenty miles to the nearest town to get any parts you've forgotten, much less gas or oil—or sometimes a much-needed utility trailer.

And when you're a Christian, living sometimes "on a wing and a prayer" as an old saying goes, God seems to show His mercy more abundantly to those who have that little grain of faith... because they lack the real know-how of worldly solutions.

"Holy Ground" indeed...

Despite the recent popularity of zero-turn riding lawnmow-ers, the Lord seemed to provide the chance to purchase, more cheaply, a one-owner regular riding lawnmower in the city across the river and in the next county. All I had to do was get there with cash to pay. And I did.

It was a proud sight for me the day I drove off from that pur-chase with the mower in the bed of my old 300,000-mile pickup truck—ready for anything, most men would say... or at least it would appear so. Kind of like the look and feel of you in your four-wheel drive, complete with hunting vehicle atop the bed. Made you feel like a secure, reasonable and capable man.

So much for being capable.

Because soon it was more of a sad sight, later at home on the river, with my neighbors directing me down my back yard hill toward my river frontage, urging me to reverse, then back up, fast and hard, in order to get "just the right angle" to enable me to get my mower out of the bed and on land. The idea of borrowing a utility trailer had escaped my enthusiastic, manly mind.

An hour later, still no progress had been made. I was embarrassed. The hill was too steep, and the river was too close and dangerous for even a seemingly-bold man like myself to push that envelope.

Perception is reality, they say. And I knew from the look in my neighbors' eyes the perception they were feeling about me.Problem was, there was no "backing out" of a heavenly-designed "Holy Ground" situation being constructed for the "building up of my faith," to quote Scripture. But if not attained, this day's failure would remain a constant reminder of my inadequacy.

I reasoned... well, the mower would not be disembarked from my pickup bed, number one.

And number two, even though the "so what" guy inside my head thought I could still soldier on, despite the problem, I was beginning to realize that in the future I would be known as the man who keeps his riding mower in his pickup bed.

A symbol of my manliness... or inadequacy? Let's just call it the Christian life.

Can I get an "Amen"?

God to my rescue...

The last "rational" moment I recall that afternoon was turning toward a neighbor, who was shaking her head at my dilemma, and getting into the driver's seat. The first "spiritual" moment I recall was racing the truck engine, putting it into gear and—reaching the top of the level ground by my home—proclaiming, "I'm on 'Holy Ground,' Jackie!"

The neighbor's look was priceless. And I can imagine the look down from above from the Lord, with a nod of approval. After all, the Scripture says, "without faith, it's impossible to please God," I had learned. Just to power up the situation, I threw in a little boast about the Lord—which couldn't hurt, I thought. "I'm gonna get this mower on the ground, with God's help!"

I tore out of the driveway, heading down that dusty, clay wash-board, rutted River Road, passing homes new and old, with cars and pickups owned by my old and young neighbors, living peaceful lives without interruption by an errant Christian man needing a God-sent miracle. *My neighbors can't help me… well, there you go,* I thought.

I can assure you that I had no thought of who would help me now, or how, and it was a bit of relaxation for my busy brain. And it was my most recent "leap of faith," which someone of my emotional tendencies is prone to do.

But as I kept driving—going nowhere in particular—I heard it.

The sound of hammers and electric saws came from the back of a house where some construction-type young men were as-sembling a new riverfront porch. My truck actually seemed to turn itself into the drive, or maybe it was unabashed hope. Not caring, I jumped from the driver's side and headed to the back yard to talk with folks I'd never seen before.

"You don't know me, but I need your help," I yelled above the sounds of their progress. And the entire silly story flowed out as these five guys just looked, and apparently wondered: Who was this problematic man, and where did he come from?"Let's help this man out," a young contractor interrupted. He was evidently the crew boss, and they soon gathered in the front yard, setting up boards and grappling with the ignition of the mower, still up in the truck bed. And, as is sometimes the case with engine protocol, the engine flooded. Go figure.

Engine locked…

And now the mower, even with the boards and know-how to safely drive it down their ramp – couldn't work. The engine had locked.

But I'm on 'Holy Ground,' I thought to the Lord, the orchestrator of all good things in my life.

This off-brand riding mower was actually pretty big, as are most problems I have faced in my journey with God. Ah… but the strength of these several men to surround the truck bed, lifting it up, over, and down to the ground, was greater.

"Holy Ground" completed. It was God.

My thanks to these guys, at least in my mind, was soon akin to a scene from the movie *Patton*, where the general saluted and pinned the praise on worthy troops after a miraculous victory in Europe. They must have thought me strange.

So, I drove my truck home, and then walked back a while later to the house where the crew were back in the rear of the home, working as if nothing strangely out-of-the-ordinary had happened.

This time, my mower started with no flooded engine, which made me smile. And I waved—looking above—and wondering at the sight the Lord saw that day: strangers, a truck, and a no-way-out-of-this Christian's problem.

My wife later said that I should have tried to bring pizza, sandwiches, a fish fry—anything—to these men a day or so afterward, to show appreciation for that heavenly job well done.

Well, I need to do that. Still haven't, though… been busy mowing my grass.

I console myself with the thought of God's blessings that

day… for the one rescued and his rescuers… all standing for a few moments on a piece of Alabama clay that became "Holy Ground."

STEPS OF A RIGHTEOUS MAN

It's hard to sleep at night, as tomorrow seems always to be an out-of-control Spirit journey.

Eventually, though, I thank God in my bed for what He did for me that day of my salvation years ago, in a soulfully-said plea for His mercy and grace for me—just a man who yearns to know his Creator.

These days, in my sixties, wherever I walk there seems to materialize an unexpected "Holy Ground"—God's ground to meet with Him.

Maybe these really are the last days before His return. I try to take solace in that.

Sometimes in this world, we are tempted to think that life could be summed up in the Avicii song "Wake Me Up When It's All Over." The song expresses a need for purpose, a need for meaning, a need for wisdom. It questions being lost.

But I know that I'm saved—and, in fact, purposefully made for these times of faith rather than feelings, spirit rather than physical, God rather than, well... me.

God help me. Truly. Can I get an "Amen"?

Recently, God mercifully reminded me of my purpose: to glorify Him in all things. And this was a miracle.

Was I alone? Not really...

Taking my young border collie to the farm one afternoon this past winter seemed like good conditioning for his future herding confidence, and other than him, I was alone on hundreds of acres… searching for my small herd of beef cows and hoping that my dog could become their new experience with man.

In my life I've been seemingly alone in many awkward situations, and this day was no different as I forged ahead, running and pointing toward the cows, urging my dog Garrett to "get 'em."

It had been raining, and the hills seemed higher than normal, and the muck in the valleys more grasping of the loose boots that I wore. Pasture typography should be considered by farmers, especially in this case—and this one farmer was running straight downhill, but his eyes were entirely to his left, leading his own "charge of the light brigade," to borrow from a similarly audacious event from my history books.

I just didn't see the downed trees between me and my brood cow herd gathered in the distance. I remember looking toward my dog with a yell of encouragement—but then it happened. A large log caught my left foot, and my speed catapulted me forward to unseen ground and unknown water, mud… and near unconsciousness.

It seems trite to say that the events moved in slow motion, but they did—well, the ones I remember. My right forearm hit something hard, and I bounced forward and then to my left, slamming my face against another log. My mouth hurt like the dickens. Then I stopped and just lay there.

Afraid to move, I asked God to help me. Afraid my teeth had been knocked out, I was rapturously elated when I felt and found that they were there. But my face was numb, as if I had hit a wall. I managed to get to my feet.

Arm and face torn up, a rib cracked, but teeth intact, I turned to run home to safety—wherever that really was. I didn't know exactly, but I knew that my truck was about a half a mile away, up one hill and on a plateau near the hay pen. I ran, then walked and breathed… and suddenly, there was Garrett bounding by me.

Then a thought hit me like another fall. "Where are your glasses?"

I knew it was the Lord, but I was through—"done," as they say. Forget farming, forget cows, bulls, dogs, fields, hay, and cute newborn calves "skipping" in the spring, as the Bible says—a sight not enough people are fortunate to see. Still, I was hurt, and I knew it. I kept walking.

"But God …," to quote Scripture, in His persistent Holy Spirit, slowed me down with a command. "Go back."

"Right," I replied to God, sarcastically. "I'll find my truck, hope the dog follows, and get help to come back and search that end of the pasture." Next problem: I couldn't see clearly six feet ahead of me, due to my nearsightedness. Well… He turned me around against my will. But "where the Spirit leads," as the Word says.

Good luck! I thought.

Walking back down that hill to the valley of muck and downed trees, the possibility of finding my glasses seemed almost laughable. By now, I had calmed down enough to realize that I couldn't even drive my truck successfully without them.

In front of me was all a blur. Truly, it was in the Lord's hands.

Who always knows? God…

Not remembering, and truly not seeing, where I had run—or fallen—there was no "clear" evidence to me of a fall or two in this large bayou of water and wet land. And yes, the cows were on the other side looking at me—I could make them out. Who knows where Garrett was; I didn't care anymore, as there was no way out of this except for God to find the glasses that He saw and knew where they had gone. I didn't even remember for sure if I had them on during my crazy run.

Sometimes, no words can adequately express the meaning behind some portions of Scripture, I believe, except to the spiritually attuned—and this biblically miraculous event was happening to me. It is still unexplained in my mind today.

God guided me—not wavering six yards, six feet, or even six inches to the left or right, and going down that long hill by His steps that I did not choose. Totally led by the Spirit, I stopped, or was stopped, in an area that seemed eerily familiar, yet like just another bog of water and mud. Prompted to suddenly look down in the blurriness, I then got on my hands and knees within a foot of that quagmire. There, sticking out of the muddy water, were two little sticks which I could see near a log. They were the backs of my glasses.

Amazing? Never in my life was there such an unreal sight.

I grabbed at what I saw—where only three inches of these "sticks" was visible—and pulled them up. A miracle!

"Jehovah! Thank You, Jehovah. You found them and guided my footsteps," I yelled across the pasture at the top of my lungs. If I had had some stones, no fooling, I would have built an altar even Abraham would have been proud of.

I was still alone there, however, except for God and the cows. Heaven knows where Garrett was.

My dog appeared, probably because of all of the screaming, and we walked back to the truck over the next hill to the slope by the hay pen.

Driving back to that portion of pasture the next day—this time walking around thoughtfully, wearing my glasses—I could see no evidence of the one particularly large puddle where the discovery was made. There was nothing different about any of what I saw. It was still water-flooded land, with several large logs strewn about in the trees of that gully. But it was now drying up a little. Amazing.

No evidence also of the many divinely guided steps of a man traumatized by a fall he didn't see coming. About an acre or three of muck, in a pasture of 266. And by now, the cows had moved on to the next valley.

There's just no way to explain it, and God is the only witness I have. Truly, it was His meeting with me in my "Holy Ground" time of trouble.

To God be the glory for giving me "the steps of a righteous man," according to Scripture.

My steps—those of a sinner made righteous by faith in Jesus Christ—literally were "ordered by the Lord."

"HOLY GROUNDS" IN YOUR LIFE?

The more time that my wife and I spend together, the more our expressions and reactions mirror each other. And that "likeness" makes us, who look very opposite—as much as a Brit and a Scott can be—at times tend to be the mirror image of the other.

As Christians, being transformed "into the image" of the Father Creator is not only a surety, but a directive. We can feel confident that "he who hath seen me hath seen the Father," as Jesus said. So, add your name there.

The challenge is in "how" we see things, and whose eyes we are using to view these sometimes dastardly-timed events, of which we are to be witnesses.

Your eyes/heart connection...

I've known some would-be saints who saw life as the world sees it, living in the power of their own minds and trusting in goodness to prevail somehow.

I've also known others who were like a song's lyrics stated in the 1990s: "the saints are just the sinners/we fall down and get up" to fight the good fight of faith, as the apostle Paul referenced in Scripture.

The miraculous happens throughout history, wherever sinners beat their breasts in contrition, and find their spiritual eyes enlightened. They view the world like a converted Saint Patrick, Martin Luther—or in recent decades, D. L. Moody or Billy Graham. That redeemed list goes on.

These, and many others in history, took on the sufferings of Christ, and in their newfound sight developed empathy toward non-Christians and Christians especially… regarding the evil "that so easily besets us," as Scripture states.

Christ as our viewfinder…

And while our daily quiet times bring us closer to God, it is the afterward walk by faith and not by our sight that is telling.

That faith can give us the mind of Christ, the fellowship of His sufferings… and the eyes which made Him not only the Redeemer, but also a "man of sorrows and acquainted with grief."

Compassion, empathy, and empowered living are the result.

The Bible, the *Passion of the Christ* film, and *The Purpose Driven Life* book may have slowed my daily "journey" speedometer down to a walk. My deeper sense is that I began seeing with new eyes the world in which I have been placed. I'm hoping in faith that these few chapters about my personal "Holy Ground" experiences have attempted to link you more closely to your true teacher, God's Holy Spirit, and away from man's wisdom… even your own.

Interestingly, you'll find yourself being alone, in a way like Jesus, who often separated Himself from others to commune with the Father. But we're not Jesus, I know.

Neither was Moses, when God's directive was an audible command to take off his shoes… as he was standing on his biblical "Holy Ground."

A closer relationship…

These awesome, even frightening events, when God—or His messengers—appear to us personally, are His validation of a closer relationship with you.

Embrace these times—these "Holy Grounds"—where God sends you a word of knowledge, gives you tongues of other men or of angels, imparts healing or even raising from the dead. For some, like myself, you'll be rescued again and again. Sweet times.

Do you want "Holy Grounds" in your life? They come at a price.

First, a personal acceptance of Christ's blood, shed at a place called Calvary as the true sacrificial Lamb, making peace with the Father. As a line from Joni Mitchell's "Woodstock" song of my youth implores: "We've got to get ourselves back to the Garden."

Second comes a realization of your extreme need for more of God as our Creator, Savior, Redeemer, Healer, Provider, Master, Comforter and Friend. Hallelujah!

Then, look around your new life with His eyes, and back at your "Holy Grounds" of communion with God. What a merciful God, to give you these!

By the way… There are many more ahead, like every good and perfect gift He has in store for you who draw near to Him.

It's a wonderful journey, this Christian life. And when God shows up… everything changes!

Psalm 34:19 (KJV)

"Many are the afflictions of the righteous: but the Lord delivereth him out of them all."

JBB

CPSIA information can be obtained
at www.ICGtesting.com
Printed in the USA
LVHW040057071020
668072LV00005B/491

9 781647 733544